RAHAB

Also by Olajumoke Adenowo

Non-Fiction

Child of Destiny

Covenant Forces

Life Spring (The Mother's Prayer Manual)

Designed for Marriage

Mysterious Seed

Appointment with Destiny

Fiction

Beyond My Dreams

RAHAB

WISDOM FOR A QUANTUM CHANGE
(BOOK ONE)

KINGDOM DYNAMICS FOR THE MARKETPLACE

OLAJUMOKE ADENOWO

Kingdom Dynamics for the Marketplace (Book One)

RAHAB: Wisdom for a Quantum Change

ISBN 978-978-57390-0-8

Book Production & Design:
Infospektra Publishing

Unless otherwise indicated, all scriptures are taken from the King James Version (KJV).

CONTENTS

INTRODUCTION

I am privileged through God's grace to function in many major roles. Two of these are quite dear to my heart and roles I am actively and passionately involved in and identified with around the globe. I am:

- an architect who, by the grace of God, is internationally recognized in my profession, and
- a minister of the gospel and member of the International Coalition of Apostolic Leaders.

While I realize that for most Christians, consciously or unconsciously, a divide has been created between ministry and the marketplace, it is God's desire that His Kingdom covers the earth, including its structures and operating systems, and the entire cosmos. As much as we may be powerful juggernauts in our fellowships and religious assemblies, the Lord wants us to wield His influence and effect His transformation in our workplace and wherever He has assigned us to function.

Dear child of God, praying and believing alone will not make this happen. There are principles and Kingdom truths we have to learn, believe, and live out to take our places in our world as God designed. I intend to reveal and mine these powerful nuggets from an unusual source: the lives of Rahab, Ruth, and Tamar, three remarkable women listed in the lineage of Jesus in the first chapter of Matthew in the Bible.

As with every other woman listed in that chapter, we find these women took extraordinary decisions, led unusual lives, and had peculiar stories which altered their trajectories, affected their communities, and changed the course of history. Indeed, we may argue that their recognition amongst men despite being in patriarchal societies was because of their uniqueness, and probably the Lord's desire for us to learn from and pay specific attention to them.

This is my hope for this series, that barriers of gender, race, age, tribe, and tongue will fail to keep you from the constellation of stars in your generation as you follow the principles these women followed. I pray that the truths revealed would cause a quantum metamorphosis and a palpable and radical alteration which can be measured and seen in you, causing you to institute the transformation you were designed to birth. May you be remembered amongst men and may your life be unquestionably lifted forever.

By faith the harlot Rahab perished not with them that believed not, when she had received the spies with peace.

Heb. 11:31

Chapter 1

AN OVERVIEW

And Joshua the son of Nun sent out of Shittim two men to spy secretly, saying, Go view the land, even Jericho. And they went, and came into an harlot's house, named Rahab, and lodged there.
Josh. 2:1

We live in a world where value is placed by many on wealth and earthly possessions. Each day, it appears man's role upon awaking is to strive tirelessly to acquire as much as one possibly can. The purpose? Majorly, to influence others and wield a measure of power in different spheres of life. But Kingdom folk are governed by different principles. Our purpose each day is to wake up to His desire and assignment, constantly asking, 'What will God have me do today?'

But seek ye first the kingdom of God, and his righteousness; and all these things shall be added unto you.
Matt. 6:33

We are instructed by God to be wise and focus on what He has called us to, and everything else about life subsequently would fall in place. We are to live with the consciousness that we are ambassadors of the Kingdom, and all the benefits of being Heaven's representative accrue to us.

We are to live with the consciousness that we are ambassadors of the Kingdom, and all the benefits of being Heaven's representative accrue to us.

The natural, earthly ambassador is privy to many benefits **while carrying out his duties.** Some of these include:

- access to the very best and all the perks of his country irrespective of the state of the country to which he is assigned.
- the best protection. Efforts are made to ensure he has the best defence and is carefully guarded considering he is the responsibility of the country sending him forth.
- diplomatic immunity within the country to which he is assigned.

In examining these few points, do you see a parallel between the natural ambassador and the believer resident here on the earth? These same privileges and more apply to us, and we are to live each day focused on the Father's will knowing we are perfectly and completely cared for. That is God's desire.

Doing the will of the Father is wisdom. Wisdom is rare. Wisdom sets apart and distinguishes. If we all had the same strategy in a race, a strategy predicated on the same information, it would be difficult to gain any competitive advantage. To get ahead in any field or in the race of life, we must have access to hidden wisdom which fellow competitors do not possess.

Wisdom can be found in the most unlikely places. One example is seen in Psalms 8:2 -

Out of the mouth of babes and sucklings hast thou ordained strength because of thine enemies, that thou mightest still the enemy and the avenger.

Why would God choose babes to reveal strength? I guess it is to make His wisdom only accessible to a few who are humble and meek, and not too proud to receive from infants. The proud would despise such lowly sources and miss the wisdom concealed and its resultant opportunities. Only those humble enough to stoop, physically stoop as is usually necessary when wanting to listen to babes, would have access to the wisdom God has ordained in their mouths. This principle is seen playing out over and over again all through scriptures.

One such example which I would want us to explore and which I hope you are humble enough to learn from is the unusual story of Rahab.

Let's read through our story in scriptures:

And Joshua the son of Nun sent out of Shittim two men to spy secretly, saying, Go view the land, even Jericho. And they went, and came into an harlot's house, named Rahab, and lodged there. And it was told the king of Jericho, saying, Behold, there came men in hither to night of the children of Israel to search out the country. And the king of Jericho sent unto Rahab, saying, Bring forth the men that are come to thee, which are entered into thine house: for they be come to search out all the country.

And the woman took the two men, and hid them, and said thus, There came men unto me, but I wist not whence they were: And it came to pass about the time of shutting of the gate, when it was dark, that the men went out: whither the men went I wot not: pursue after them quickly; for ye shall overtake them. But she had brought them up to the roof of the house, and hid them with the stalks of flax, which she had laid in order upon the roof. And the men pursued after them the way to Jordan unto the fords: and as soon as they which pursued after them were gone out, they shut the gate.

And before they were laid down, she came up unto them upon the roof; And she said unto the men, I know that the LORD hath given you the land, and that your terror is fallen upon us, and that all the inhabitants of the land faint because of you. For we have heard how the LORD dried up the water of the Red sea for you, when ye came out of Egypt; and what ye did unto the two kings of the Amorites, that were on the other side Jordan, Sihon and Og, whom ye utterly destroyed. And as soon as we had heard these things, our hearts did melt, neither did there remain any more courage in any man, because of you: for the LORD your God, he is God in heaven above, and in earth beneath.

To get ahead in any field or indeed in the race of lifewe must have access to hidden wisdom which fellow competitors do not possess.

Now therefore, I pray you, swear unto me by the LORD, since I have shewed you kindness, that ye will also shew kindness unto my father's house, and give me a true token: And that ye will save alive my father, and my mother, and my brethren, and my sisters, and all that they have, and deliver our lives from death.

And the men answered her, Our life for yours, if ye utter not this our business. And it shall be, when the LORD hath given us the land, that we will deal kindly and truly with thee. Then she let them down by a cord through the window: for her house was upon the town wall, and she dwelt upon the wall. And she said unto them, Get you to the mountain, lest the pursuers meet you; and hide yourselves there three days, until the pursuers be returned: and afterward may ye go your way.

And the men said unto her, We will be blameless of this thine oath which thou hast made us swear. Behold, when we come into the land, thou shalt bind this line of scarlet thread in the window which thou didst let us down by: and thou shalt bring thy father, and thy mother, and thy brethren, and all thy father's household, home unto thee.

And it shall be, that whosoever shall go out of the doors of thy house into the street, his blood shall be upon his head, and we will be guiltless: and whosoever shall be with thee in the house, his blood shall be on our head, if any hand be upon him. And if thou utter this our business, then we will be quit of thine oath which thou hast made us to swear.

And she said, According unto your words, so be it. And she sent them away, and they departed: and she bound the scarlet line in the window. And they went, and came unto the mountain, and abode there three days, until the pursuers were returned: and the pursuers sought them throughout all the way, but found them not.

So the two men returned, and descended from the mountain, and passed over, and came to Joshua the son of Nun, and told him all things that befell them: And they said unto Joshua, Truly the LORD hath delivered into our hands all the land; for even all the inhabitants of the country do faint because of us.

Josh. 2:1-24

I would like us to explore these chapters and glean lessons that apply to our walk in our world today as every facet of the story above is very revealing. These would be lessons we can practically deploy effectively and whose outcomes we can measure as men and women in our lives and in the marketplace.

The story begins in Joshua 2:1:

And Joshua the son of Nun sent out of Shittim two men to spy secretly, saying, Go view the land, even Jericho. And they went, and came into an harlot's house, named Rahab, and lodged there.

Let's pause here for a moment. This starts to get interesting. The name of the harlot into whose house they come is Rahab. In ancient times, like in much of Africa and the orient, people are named purposefully. Names can either be prophetic - what the parents or caregivers hope for, believe, and pray that the children become – or determined by the circumstances of their birth like Jabez whose mother named him 'Sorrow' or Ichabod whose mother named him 'The glory of the Lord has departed.'

And Jabez was more honourable than his brethren: and his mother called his name Jabez, saying, Because I bare him with sorrow.

1 Chron. 4:9

And she named the child Ichabod, saying, The glory is departed from Israel: because the ark of God was taken, and because of her father in law and her husband.

1 Sam. 4:21

Rahab, sometimes spelled Rachab, was given a name which when interpreted in the Hebrew language meant Expansion, Spaciousness, and Enlargement. What were her parents' dreams when they had her? Why was she given the name? Was it their wish for her, that her coast would be enlarged, her territory increase, and her influence spread far and wide? Did they envision for her a great destiny? We can be sure, like every parent, they wanted the best for their daughter Rahab and as such named her accordingly.

We should not corrupt our divine restlessness with envy when we see people functioning in our 'patterns' or in ways in which we perceive God wants us to.

But while she bore the name Rahab, the

circumstances of her life gave her another label – Harlot. As depicted in scripture, she was recognised and identified by these two titles 'Harlot' and 'Rahab (Expansion, Spaciousness, and Enlargement)' on a regular basis, consciously and unconsciously. While she might have coasted along, uncaring what she was called, time would present to her the opportunity to choose which of these she would be remembered by and what her legacy would be.

We all have a choice, between what our destinies call us *up to* or what the circumstances of life want to drag us *down into*. We have a choice between being remembered for a legacy chosen by God or being defined by our pain. Rahab's actions and responses in the story read were a reflection of the conflict and battle present within her.

We have a choice between being remembered for our legacy or being defined by our pain.

I empathise because perhaps, like me, you have also had seasons where you have actually been driven to despair by prophecies which have been spoken over you, good prophecies which belie your present circumstances. You have done all you know to do, prayed, fasted, and prayed some more. But nothing seems to be changing. Do not despair, you are not alone.

Sometimes, really, there's nothing more to do than stand and keep standing in faith with an attitude of unalloyed worship, in full submission to His will. Having done all to stand, we stay standing in patience as we continue to worship.

Even in despair, we do not forget that these prophecies stand as testaments and witnesses to the divine will, and as such they still remain the goal. I pray that some of the principles in this book, as simple as they may seem, will be the bridge(s) between prophecy and fulfilment for you.

We each have a purpose designed for us from before our creation by God.

And now, O Father, glorify thou me with thine own self with the glory which I had with thee before the world was.

Joh. 17:5

We all have a glory received from God before time began. God created each one for a definite purpose, with each sitting on a unique throne. Our thrones differ and the expressions of our glory differ. Therefore, we are not meant to compare ourselves to others but rather to God's plan for us.

For we dare not make ourselves of the number, or compare ourselves with some that commend themselves: but they measuring themselves by themselves, and comparing themselves among themselves, are not wise.

2 Cor. 10:12

As a three-year-old, I would wonder where I had been before I was born, and adults would tell me I was "in Heaven." I never felt my question had been adequately answered until the day I heard within me, "*Before you were born you were a dream in My heart.*" Before we were born on this earth, we were each God's dream and are each God's idea. The choice is and will always be yours to decide which image to embrace: that from God and His Word or that foisted on you by others.

If we do not honour those who have gone before us into the operations we seek, we close our access to the gates of these realms they operate in.

No matter what led you here or what you have been made to become, even when you may not fully understand what you are called to or who you are meant to be, like Rahab may have experienced from a young age, God would present glimpses of the life for which you were designed and the path you are meant to take. These pointers may stem from an inexplicable restlessness, or an agitation when we see people functioning on platforms or in realms we know we should be functioning in.

It is, however, pertinent to sound a note of warning at this point. We should not corrupt our divine restlessness with envy when we see people functioning in our 'patterns' or in ways in which we perceive God wants us to. Instead, we should let their successes provoke and encourage us to strive for more, even as we honour them for what God is doing in their lives. If we do not honour those who have gone before us into the operations we seek, we close our access to the gates of these realms they operate in.

Rahab's story has baffled and still baffles many. We see her move from being definitely outside God's covenant to enlarging the frontiers of her horizon, enough to take the quantum leap which would lift this Jericho prostitute from a spiritual mire and graft her into the bloodline of the Christ.

But how did she recognize the opportunity presented her, and negotiate her way to a place amongst the covenant people? Also, how does a harlot from a foreign land doomed to destruction move from a position accursed by God to becoming a mother in the lineage of Jesus?

While the believer's ability to engage in spiritual activities is very important and cannot be undermined, faith without works is dead.

For as the body without the spirit is dead, so faith without works is dead also.
Jam. 2:26

Within each chapter below we would examine Rahab's life to get a glimpse of who she was and traits she possessed which prepared and led her into the opportunity of a lifetime. While this is definitely a story of God's grace and favour, it is also the story of wisdom from which we can glean principles applicable in our marketplace which are sure to guarantee success.

Are you ready to discover these secrets? Let's begin.

Chapter 2

PRINCIPLE I
A Right Heart

And the woman took the two men, and hid them, ….
Josh. 2:4

Rahab was a harlot. The Bible does not mince words about her profession and lifestyle. As prostitution was often a part of ancient religions, there is also a high probability that she was a religious prostitute. This would have made her job and position in society prestigious. She didn't abide in the loving arms of a faithful husband while in Jericho as no husband or significant other is mentioned in her entire story.

As a harlot, it would need no stretch of the imagination to figure out she had seen the worst of men and encountered the underbelly of the male gender. In fact, if there was anything she must have learnt it would be that men couldn't be counted on to keep their vows (or so it would seem based on the conduct of her clients). Despite being used to disappointments, how then could she trust foreign Hebrew strangers she was encountering for the first time?

OPENNESS

God cannot effect changes in our lives without the agents called men. I refer to these as the human race. When it comes to our financial lives, the same principle applies.

God cannot print money in Heaven. If He does, it would make Him a criminal and a counterfeiter. That money could not be legal tender. What this means clearly is that the finances you need are in the accounts, pockets, and purses of men and women somewhere. One or some of the 7.2 billion people on Planet Earth have the cash you need, and you must encounter and interact with them one way or the other for there to be a legal transfer of their resources to you.

One or some of the 7.2 billion people on Planet Earth have the cash you need, and you must encounter and interact with them one way or the other for there to be a legal transfer of their resources to you.

People will willingly part with

their resources when you deliver value usually in the form of solving a problem they have already identified or one you are able to help them identify. When we don't have a system by which new entrants are allowed into our sphere, we shut the door to new encounters and fresh blessings.

Permit me to use myself as an example here. In my line of business as a woman, I have no choice but to deal with the opposite gender. This I do to the best of my ability courteously and with all propriety. The economic realities in the global business climate are configured in such a way that men control most of the decisions in my field.

People will willingly part with their resources when you deliver value usually in the form of solving a problem they have already identified or one you are able to help them identify.

If you sell services, goods, and commodities to women your case may be different. Perhaps your most significant interactions with men would be for financial services. Women in male-dominated industries like mine (Architecture) are faced with a totally different set of realities which are difficult to comprehend from the outside, and are not the subject of this discourse.

My point, however, is if we are suspicious of everyone we encounter or do not retain the right perspective in dealing with each one we meet, we won't be open to or make room for new opportunities. Bear in mind that relationships that lead to business may not start off as business relationships. When trust is established, a platonic relationship may lead to a referral that will produce some of the most advantageous opportunities you have ever encountered.

I love people and love meeting people. For me, each person is like a special package gift-wrapped by God. While I don't throw discernment or caution to the wind in dealing with each one, I choose to believe everyone is innocent until proven guilty. Rahab's openness saved her family, placed her on her throne, and gave her a legacy for all eternity.

FORGIVENESS

There are some who have decided not to ever trust again because of past hurts. While we can be more cautious as we allow past experiences to teach us, we would have failed the test if we shut the doors of our lives to people generally or a certain class of people because certain members of their ilk hurt us in the past.

It is often said in politics and in the marketplace that there are no permanent relationships, only permanent interests. Some understand this and are able to compartmentalize their goals and interests in business, governance, or politics.

Others, however, seem to transfer personal sentiments to business dealings. Women especially.

It is often said that in the marketplace and politics, there are no permanent relationships, only permanent interests.

A lot of women do not get along with women who are in positions at the moment that can yield great benefits not just for themselves, but for their community. They refuse to relate and cooperate with the other because some little thing has gotten in the way, usually petty, ephemeral, having no lasting value, and typically some perceived slight on the self-esteem.

In business you must stay discerning and be quick to let go of real or imagined slights, hurts, and petty issues in the overriding interest. I am really saddened when I see female entrepreneurs or women in the marketplace refuse to deal with other women over a perceived slight or offence. When asked why oftentimes, some relay stories which have spanned decades. Some of these stories may not even directly involve the speaker. "Her Aunt took my Aunt's second husband," or some story really irrelevant to the transaction at hand!

Let's learn to Forgive! Unforgiveness is a self-made prison. This is as true in business relationships as it is in other types of relationships. If I may quote a character (Kaniz) from my work of fiction *Beyond My Dreams*, "Whoever hurt you, don't make *me* pay for his sins." We shouldn't make new people God is sending our way pay for the sins of those who hurt us in the past. If we do not forgive and move on, pretty soon we will have no one left to do business with.

Chapter 3

PRINCIPLE II
Discernment

And she said unto the men, I know that the LORD hath given you the land, and that your terror is fallen upon us, and that all the inhabitants of the land faint because of you.

Josh. 2:9

Rahab was able to recognize the difference between these men and the run-of-the-mill potential clients who frequented her digs. For a prostitute, there's only one thing you would expect men want from you. So how did she know these two men did not want the same thing? Discernment. This is the ability to tell the difference between one from another, and the critical X-factor that allows us engage new people without opening our lives to danger, hurt, abuse, and other undesirable experiences.

All men may be equal in creation, but what each has made of the life God handed them has distinguished them from the other.

There is one glory of the sun, and another glory of the moon, and another glory of the stars: for one star differeth from another star in glory.

1 Cor. 15:41

We are all stars but with differing glory. Dare I say we are always manifesting the glory in varying degrees in differing seasons? Therefore, only God, who created humans and their times and seasons of manifestation, can decode what the package who stands before you really contains in any season. We must have that gift that Rahab had - the ability to discern one person from another.

Those who are graced to discern value quickly and relate to people from this place of understanding have a head start in the race of life.

Accurately discerning each human being is the first key to unlocking the blessings they each carry and accessing their gifting. We must be cautious about defining what discernment really is though. Some think they have a gift of discernment, but they are just naturally overly suspicious.

All people are not the same in every situation or at all times. While we may be equal in God, we are not equal in grace, not equal in skill, and not equal in the value we bring to each life. Those who are graced to discern value quickly and relate to people from this place of understanding have a head start in the race of life.

Promotion lies in discerning the difference in each person you meet or terrain you find yourself. Some people are doors that lead to other opportunities, some are windows that provide insight to horizons you never knew existed, and some are walls - they lead nowhere, obstruct you, and are barriers in your life. In practical terms, some clients are doors that lead to other doors, and some potential clients might be time wasters. The ability to discern who is what is really key. Assess relationships and situations carefully and determine which is a door, a window, or a wall.

We honour human beings essentially because of the principle of Potential Difference. This is the distinguishing factor between one person and another. I have taught on this principle which I learnt in physics classes. The blessing or anointing is a form of energy, and energy flows from a region of higher potential to one of lower potential. At the point of receiving the blessing therefore, no matter how highly a person perceives himself to be, you must assume a posture lower than that of the giver for transference to occur.

And without all contradiction the less is blessed of the better.
Heb. 7:7

Water, energy, and oil do not flow upwards. They flow downwards. It takes humility to honour others so that the blessings embedded within them can flow down to you. Rahab gave due honour to the spies after she had accurately discerned who they were, and she accessed the blessing they carried.

Chapter 4

PRINCIPLE III
Discretion

And the men answered her, Our life for yours, if ye utter not this our business. And it shall be, when the LORD hath given us the land, that we will deal kindly and truly with thee.
Josh. 2:14

Rahab possessed this important attribute. She was very discreet. She did not discuss the business with the spies with anyone. While she pondered what their arrival meant and what it could mean for the city, she went about her business maintaining sealed lips. On the other hand, however, others with the same knowledge thought being wise was running off to the palace with the information of the spies' arrival, in a bid to curry favour from the king.

In many professions, discretion is key. This is applied in my profession as an architect. I never discuss my clients. While this is common behaviour in our society and considered a way to boost your public persona before others, boasts about projects one has undertaken for various people should be avoided. People are looking for those who can be trusted in the field of business. A discreet person will be treasured above someone who tells all.

If we want to be exposed to high-level transactions we must learn to be discreet, and this applies especially to the female folk. In many traditional societies, women are believed not to be able to retain secrets. So many ancient cults exclude them as a result. We should learn to disappoint the prediction that women cannot be trusted.

Rahab kept the agreement with the spies to herself. An Angela Merkel (Chancellor of Germany) or a Theresa May (erstwhile Prime minister of the United Kingdom) must learn to keep private the intentions of her party and those of different stakeholders at the helm of affairs if she is going to move the country forward.

If we want to be exposed to high level transactions, we must learn to be discreet...

Irrespective of your gender, don't be one given to much speech. If you have to speak, avoid talking about people and revealing secrets. Be watchful. By the time you begin to mention names, the discussion has moved from mere conversation to gossip. There is so much to discuss as mature individuals seeking to make an impact in our various fields; ideas are the real focus of the great.

Is it possible people are not entrusting you with high-level transactions because they do not trust you to keep private what they term confidential?

Chapter 5

PRINCIPLE IV
Wisdom

And it was told the king of Jericho, saying, Behold, there came men in hither tonight of the children of Israel to search out the country. And the king of Jericho sent unto Rahab, saying, Bring forth the men that are come to thee, which are entered into thine house: for they be come to search out all the country. And the woman took the two men, and hid them, and said thus, There came men unto me, but I wist not whence they were.

Josh. 2:2–4

Wisdom loosely translated is the right application of knowledge. Rahab expressed this principle in a number of ways. Let's consider a few.

UNDERSTANDING HISTORICAL EVENTS

For we have heard how the LORD dried up the water of the Red sea for you, when ye came out of Egypt; and what ye did unto the two kings of the Amorites, that were on the other side Jordan, Sihon and Og, whom ye utterly destroyed.

Josh. 2:10

I will say something very important here: pick your opponents carefully. The secret of victory is knowing what battles to fight. It is unwise to go up against individuals or systems without the express direction and backing of the Lord. Recklessness can lead to destruction.

When the spies came to Rahab and she discovered who they were, she had many options. She could have chosen to rebel against the God of the Israelites like the rest of the city, despite the stories shared about Him. She could also have chosen to attack and instigate others against the spies. But she recalled all she had heard about their God and chose a different approach.

It is unwise to go up against individuals or systems without the express direction and backing of the Lord.

The verse above shows that all of Jericho had access to this body of knowledge Rahab remembered: the mighty works of Jehovah on behalf of the Israelites. However, she alone made the right decision based on this general knowledge or information. Isn't it amazing the events she referred to? These occurrences had happened over 40 years before her encounter with the spies. Yet, she remembered and understood history and how it influenced the present.

As business owners, we should understand the history of our industry and seismic changes taking place around the world today in comparison with changes which have happened in the past. The industrial revolution of old was no less of a seismic shift than the technological and internet revolution that we are going through now. It changed everything: the way women were viewed in the workplace, the role of children, and the dynamics of the family. It changed the way the world was seen completely.

The industrial revolution also shifted wealth from extractive economies to processing economies and changed the wealth of nations. Some nations advanced rapidly than others. Nations with natural resources ceased to be wealthy while nations that processed raw materials began to push the limit. As a result, African countries like Nigeria and Ghana which owned natural resources became impoverished while countries who profited greatly were the ones who processed these natural resources and sent them back to Africa.

One example is crude oil. All the derivative goods from its production – petroleum, kerosene, petroleum jelly, diesel, and so many other by-products – are resold to us. The nations from which the crude is extracted at great cost to the environment are not the nations that benefit the most from its production.

Learning and studying relevant history is important. We must learn about historical events and their importance even if it is not an academic requirement to do so. Do you know history pertinent to your field?

A good knowledge of history is also important because some history is cyclical. Things that have happened before happen again. Like recessions and property market booms, there are industry patterns that we can observe. Wise people are able to observe and analyse seemingly random occurrences and find the connector between these random events.

CONCERNING TIMES AND SEASONS

And as soon as we had heard these things, our hearts did melt, neither did there remain any more courage in any man, because of you: for the LORD your God, he is God in heaven above, and in earth beneath.

Josh. 2:11

Rahab was able to tell that Jericho's empire was coming to an end. She could see from the victory streak that the Israelites maintained that it was Jericho's turn to fall. This was irrespective of present realities: it is commonly held as true that the breadth of its wall was 18-feet-wide (which was accurate considering she was able to build a house on it). This was how fortified the walls were. While there was no known technology at that time to break down such a wall, yet she could tell that whatever supernatural force had led the kings of the Amorites, Sihon, and Og, to fall to these people would come through for them again when it came to Jericho.

As a business owner, you should understand the times. Learn about the future so you decide what new venture to undertake and ready your infrastructure and team for a technological leapfrog. There are many businesses that are being done today that are projected to become obsolete in the next 10-20 years; jobs like data-entry keyers, cashiers, petrol station attendants, telemarketers, travel agents.

You need to up-skill, upgrade, do whatever you need to do to prepare for the future. How perceptive are you about new trends and forecasts in your business? Are you doing all you can to stay on the cutting edge of new trends in your industry and not be taken unawares? Learn to read trends and forecast.

If you want to invest in a petroleum refinery, you have to begin to understand what the advent of electric cars will mean to you. Instead of petrol stations, should you be investing in car-charging terminals? In my short life, I have seen rotary phones give way to analogue hand-held phones and analogue hand-held phones to digital. Technology keeps advancing, and things we thought unthinkable years ago are now the norm, and all in the space of a few decades.

Like Rahab, stay perceptive. Begin to see what the future is and not just what obtains now.

CONCERNING LOYALTIES

A good knowledge of history is also important because some history is cyclical. Things that have happened before happen again.

And it was told the king of Jericho, saying, Behold, there came men in hither tonight of the children of Israel to search out the country. And the king of Jericho sent unto Rahab, saying, Bring forth the men that are come to thee, which are entered into thine house: for they be come to search out all the country.

Josh. 2:2-3

From the verse above, we can deduce Rahab was well known to the king. Perhaps he may have also been one of her clients. While this cannot be ascertained, we know she was well-positioned in her society. Yet, when she had to choose, she switched allegiance from her well-established and secure position to an uncertain one. She left the known for the unknown.

Leaders value loyalty above other virtues and are keenly interested in knowing who can be counted on. As leaders, this is key and a primal need especially when it involves going into battle. Ensuring you are safe, and knowing the right people are tasked with your security is of utmost importance. Indira Gandhi, who served as Prime Minister of India, was assassinated in October 1984 by two of her bodyguards. If there is no weakness within your circle, it is very difficult for an outsider to get through.

Leaders do not take betrayal likely at all. It is almost an unforgivable trait. We must remember, especially in business, that loyalty is key. We are to be faithful in our relationships. We are not to be disloyal or use people as stepping stones or ladders. You might get away with this in the short term but soon you will be known in the marketplace as being unreliable, selfish, and not trustworthy. When loyalty is a key factor in a transaction or business, you will be avoided like the plague.

We must remember, especially in business, that loyalty is key.

Having said this, you must be sensitive

enough to know when a leader, person, or terrain has become an enemy of God, His intents and purposes. Also, you must be sensitive enough to know when your time in a relationship has ended. Rahab understood when to switch her allegiance from the king of Jericho to the God of Israel. She understood that Jericho was now in direct opposition to God, therefore her relationship with the king, no matter how close, and her position in Jericho were over. She had to position herself for life in another dispensation.

When Rahab switched allegiance to Israel she became fully loyal to the spies and to Israel ultimately. The people among whom she dwelt had now become enemies of God, and hers also.

In the words of David in Psalm 139:21-22:

> *Do not I hate them, O Lord, that hate thee? and am not I grieved with those that rise up against thee? I hate them with perfect hatred: I count them mine enemies.*

If you insist on maintaining covenant relationships with those who rebel against God, when God chooses to judge them you stand the risk of being judged with them. This was the case with those who did not separate themselves from Korah, Dathan, and Abiram.

And the Lord spake unto Moses, saying, Speak unto the congregation, saying, Get you up from about the tabernacle of Korah, Dathan, and Abiram. And Moses rose up and went unto Dathan and Abiram; and the elders of Israel followed him. And he spake unto the congregation, saying, Depart, I pray you, from the tents of these wicked men, and touch nothing of theirs, lest ye be consumed in all their sins. So they gat up from the tabernacle of Korah, Dathan, and Abiram, on every side: and Dathan and Abiram came out, and stood in the door of their tents, and their wives, and their sons, and their little children.

And Moses said, Hereby ye shall know that the Lord hath sent me to do all these works; for I have not done them of mine own mind. If these men die the common death of all men, or if they be visited after the visitation of all men; then the Lord hath not sent me. But if the Lord make a new thing, and the earth open her mouth, and swallow them up, with all that appertain unto them, and they go down quick into the pit; then ye shall understand that these men have provoked the Lord.

And it came to pass, as he had made an end of speaking all these words, that the ground clave asunder that was under them: And the earth opened her mouth, and swallowed them up, and their houses, and all the men that appertained unto Korah, and all their goods. They, and all that appertained to them, went down alive into the pit, and the earth closed upon them: and they perished from among the congregation.

And all Israel that were round about them fled at the cry of them: for they said, Lest the earth swallow us up also. And there came out a fire from the Lord, and consumed the two hundred and fifty men that offered incense.

Numbers 16:23-35

You must be sensitive enough to know when your time in a relationship has ended.

Warn the rebellious if you are in a position to do so or instructed by the revealed or written Word to. If you cannot warn or effect a change, depart. We need to understand that some relationships are not meant to go on forever. Relationships have tenures. Some are designed for a reason, some for a season. Some are intended to be temporary and others permanent. Learn to discern each carefully.

Chapter 6

PRINCIPLE V
Industry

But she had brought them up to the roof of the house, and hid them with the stalks of flax, which she had laid in order upon the roof.

Josh. 2:6

In Proverbs 31 of the Bible, we are given a list of attributes by King Lemuel's mother found in the woman who she terms as virtuous. One core characteristic seems to encapsulate every attribute found – she is industrious. This involves being productive, hardworking, and diligent. She ran her businesses efficiently and was praised by all who knew her. The benefits accrued from her work were experienced far and wide.

While the purpose of owning a business is to be financially independent, our businesses are also meant to be platforms for us to engage the world and display the excellence of God in our lives. Engaging in transactions and rendering service to our community provide the opportunity for us to interface, engage, and ultimately influence that community.

Consider this. You are a paediatrician and a young lady brings her son to you. He is ill and she is at a vulnerable point. When you solve her immediate problem, which is her child's illness, with your medical skill and the wisdom of God in you, you gain her respect and trust and are able to speak into her life, thereby increasing and utilizing your influence for the Kingdom. This is the reason why we serve and why we do any business, that our influence and platform for the Kingdom might be broadened.

While the purpose of owning a business is to be financially independent, our businesses are also meant to be platforms for us to engage the world and display the excellence of God in our lives.

We find Rahab unconsciously exploring this Kingdom principle, and while we may argue that she does not qualify to be called a virtuous woman, yet we discover many of the attributes listed in Proverbs 31 present in her. Let's examine a few.

Attribute 1
HAVING MULTIPLE STREAMS OF INCOME

Rahab had multiple streams from which she earned her living.

1. Lodging

And Joshua the son of Nun sent out of Shittim two men to spy secretly, saying, Go view the land, even Jericho. And they went, and came into an harlot's house, named Rahab, and lodged there.

Josh. 2:1

We see the spies going into Rahab's home and lodging there. She seemed to have run an inn for those who needed a place to stay for a short while, or travellers stopping by the city.

I truly believe Rahab was very hospitable to the spies. This was the only way she would have had the privilege of not just interacting with them but becoming privy to their mission in Jericho. Being hospitable is a skill which should be found in every platform. It is your opportunity to engage the world and gives you access to influence another. Excellent service coupled with the right attitude creates an avenue for other opportunities to emerge. This attribute we find in Rahab.

In my field, my business has been my platform for reaching those who would have balked at attending a 'religious' service but who, when impressed by excellent service, trusted me to possess competencies in other areas and gave me access to more sensitive areas of their lives; and we thank God that for over 25 years in business at the time of this writing, there has been no cause for regret.

2. Catering

It is typical that most inns or lodges would provide catering services for visitors. As a result, one can safely assume Rahab provided these offerings to guests who stopped by or lodged at her inn.

3. Agriculture and Textile Production

But she had brought them up to the roof of the house, and hid them with the stalks of flax, which she had laid in order upon the roof.

Josh. 2:6

Being hospitable is a skill which should be found in every platform.

In Biblical times, flax was commonly sold or used to make linen usually, which could be worn or sold. I believe Rahab would have had farms where flax was grown. In the verse above we see she had also been involved in laying down the large flax harvest herself on the roof 'in order'. In Proverbs 31 we see a parallel:

She seeketh wool, and flax, and worketh willingly with her hands.

Prov. 31:13

Not only did Rahab deal in flax like the virtuous women, as depicted in the verse above, but she took it to another level. Her inventory was so large that it would have to be over two feet high to cover two grown men lying flat.

4. Prostitution

And Joshua the son of Nun sent out of Shittim two men to spy secretly, saying, Go view the land, even Jericho. And they went, and came into an harlot's house, named Rahab, and lodged there.

Josh. 2:1

While selling one's body for gain is not endorsed by God or recommended by this author either, it was Rahab's stock in trade and another service by which she was identified.

Many who would roundly condemn prostitution are actually, unbeknown to them, also engaged in this activity. Without condemning, validating, judging, or justifying the reasons for her actions, I feel led, perhaps for the sake of just one reader, to elaborate on what constitutes prostitution.

Let's look at the definition of a prostitute.

prostitute |*ˈprɒstɪtjuːt*|

noun:

- a person, in particular a woman, who engages in sexual activity for payment
- a person who misuses their talents or behaves unworthily for personal or financial gain

verb [with object]:

- to offer (someone) sexual activity in exchange for payment
- to put (oneself or one's talents) to an unworthy or corrupt use for personal or financial gain

We see the term is not gender-specific. It really is about trading sex, time, or valuable personal talents for any form of unworthy gain. It doesn't also have to be with unknown parties. It could even be in the context of some form of relationship. A word is enough for those who love the truth.

Attribute 2
DILIGENCE

Seest thou a man diligent in his business? he shall stand before kings; he shall not stand before mean men.

Prov. 22:29

The story is told of a young man who complained about how a colleague who had been employed after him was being promoted over him. The boss promised to respond but had an assignment for him. He said, "John, go to the market and find out if there is bottled water of pH level 7.8 available for our upcoming event." John leaves for the market and comes back an hour later to report that there is no such water available in the market.

The boss calls James, the colleague up for promotion, and tells him, "Go to the market and find out if there is bottled water of pH level 7.8 for our upcoming event." James goes immediately and reports back one hour later with his report.

"There is no water of pH Level 7.8. However, there is alkaline water of pH Level 7.79 from China, water of 7.6 alkalinity from Burundi, and water of pH level 6.5 from Portland. The water from China is bottled in reusable vessels which would concern us as we value the environment, but we can also return these bottles and get a discount on our next purchase. The water from Burundi is bottled in glasses and we would need to take special care in transporting them to the venue. Also, this option may not be safe as our guests include children. I have searched online on the water from Portland, and its pH level is not conducive for the human body. I will suggest we buy the one from China because it is easier to transport, is environmentally friendly, can be recycled, and is profitable for the organization on the next purchase."

If you had to offer either of these colleagues a job, who would you select? Diligence is key. Diligence talks about attention to detail. It carries with it the notion of reliability and consistency knowing that anytime you are called upon you can be counted on. As an employer of labour since 1994, 25 years to date, I have seen first-hand the difference diligence makes in human resource management. Bosses are keen to promote or elevate thorough people because they are usually reliable in more ways than one. Unfortunately, many people start well but do not stay diligent to the end.

Rahab's diligence, as displayed in her attention to detail and being conscientious, also played a factor in her promotion.

Ruth was noticed for her loveliness but promoted for her diligence. Also, Rahab's diligence, as displayed in her attention to detail and being conscientious, played a factor in her promotion. Your beauty, charisma, or even skill will get you noticed but will not get you promoted. Diligence carries the notion of reliability, consistency, 'firmness of constitution or character', and 'the quality of being trustworthy or of performing consistently well.'

Are there times you give your best and wonder if no one will notice? Yes. But you should be reliable enough to be counted on to do the things you should even when no one is watching. What we fail to realize is, in life most promotion comes from those who have observed us over time. We are all being watched by someone capable of promoting us. A day is coming when all you have been doing will be put to the test, and where others do not shine, you will.

Chapter 7

PRINCIPLE VI
Non-Procrastinator

Then she said, 'According to your words, so be it.' And she sent them away, and they departed. And she bound the scarlet cord in the window.
Josh. 2:21

Changes occur in times and seasons when decisive actions are taken quickly which would bring corresponding changes in your world and the earth. Rahab received clear instructions in connection with the covenant entered into and the transition which was to occur: she was to tie a scarlet thread in her window. This she did immediately.

Being able to 'tell the signs', have business proposals, feasibility studies, viability studies, and all studies are good as it is very important to count the cost and prepare for going into battle. However, when all has been said and done, you will find preparation alone will not win the battle. You must actually fight. 'Words don't cook rice' as someone says. 'Just do it'.

For everything you have left undone, someone else has gone ahead to undertake it, or it has remained undone. Know for a fact that every vision or idea received is not for your benefit alone, but also for the benefit of others. Inventions and dreams are not man's ideas. They are God's.

Every good gift and every perfect gift is from above, and cometh down from the Father of lights, with whom is no variableness, neither shadow of turning.
Jam. 1:17

These are actually not your visions but God's. He only offered the vision to you. Guess what? You may not be the only candidate being considered to execute the vision. If you don't execute it, I assure you God won't let it go till someone else does. When God is knocking on the door of your heart and you refuse to move along, He gives the dream to someone else; and guess what, it may be executed in a manner less than you would have and far from what you would like. And if you are

The world is waiting for you to manifest what God has put into you.

not careful, you might become bitter and say, "My own idea was much better." Yes, your own idea was much better but you did not execute it.

The world is waiting for you to manifest what God has put into you, and while you are busy stalling, people are suffering. If Alexander Graham Bell had not invented the telephone and nobody else had, we would still be communicating the old-fashioned way with town criers, drums, and smoke signals. No business profits the world by remaining at the stage of an idea. You must put that idea into practice, starting today, starting where you are.

A lot of people say they do not have any start-up capital. No one is asking you to start with what you don't have. In the words of Theodore Roosevelt, "Do what you can, with what you have, where you are." Do not let the perfect become the enemy of the good. While you are trying to be perfect, do not lose sight of the fact that the good you can do will benefit so many even in its imperfect state. It is time to get up and 'just do it'.

Chapter 8

PRINCIPLE VII
Skilled Negotiator

Now therefore, I pray you, swear unto me by the LORD, since I have shewed you kindness, that ye will also shew kindness unto my father's house, and give me a true token.
Josh. 2:12

Being confident and knowing what you want impacts how you are viewed as a person and business, and also determines what results you accomplish in your interactions with people you meet in the marketplace. This cannot be ignored or substituted irrespective of your skill or the sincerity of your heart.

Despite Rahab being relatively young (she married and bore children years later in the land of Israel), she was bold and confident which could be a natural result of the life she lived.

She knew what she wanted and boldly requested for it from the spies, accepting nothing less. How did she do this?

Determining Their Priority

And the king of Jericho sent unto Rahab, saying, Bring forth the men that are come to thee, which are entered into thine house: for they be come to search out all the country. And the woman took the two men, and hid them.

Josh. 2:3-4

If you are in a relationship and you are not ministering or being ministered to, it means you both have no value to add to each other.

Rahab didn't just make a request from the spies. First, she observed them and determined what they immediately needed: safety, their very *lives*. Without telling them her need, she offered them their desire first.

This principle also applies to us as individuals as we go through life. You should ask the same questions as you navigate any business or transactional terrain. *Why am I in this? Why is he in this? What does she/he want from me?*

While you know what you want, the transaction agreed to should be a win for both parties - they get what they want and you get what you want.

There should be reciprocity in every relationship. If you are in a relationship and you are not ministering or being ministered to, it means you both have no value to add to each other. You should re-evaluate the investment you want to commit to that relationship.

Well-Timed and Keen Negotiating

And before they were laid down, she came up unto them upon the roof.
Josh. 2:8

Rahab did not let the spies experience her 'goods' before she entered into negotiations with them. She waited until it was dark and the men would be getting ready to sleep and then she went up to meet them. At that point, finding a new place would have been difficult so they would have had no choice but to listen to what she had to say. Also, she had clearly demonstrated her capability to deliver what they wanted – safety.

This method was also what Estée Lauder discovered that made her a billionaire. She knew if she handed out samples and got people to try her products they would come back for more. It is also akin to giving someone a little scoop of ice-cream before allowing them buy the whole cup. Rahab applied this principle.

Don't be offended if my next words apply to you. You hand over jewellery to someone with an agreement stating she would pay later after which she wears it to an event she wants to 'shine' at. She even takes photos with your necklace, enlarges the photo, and places it in a pride of place in her house. After a while you find you have to chase her to pay you. It can run into months after the event.

What is really at play here is that she has extracted the value she desires from your goods. If she asks you to come and take them so you can stop bothering her, what is your remedy? Quite frankly, she can return them to you with no regrets. Think through your business model carefully and ask yourself always,

- At what point is value extracted and at what point do I invoice?
- If I choose to get paid after value is extracted, what are the mitigants that need to be in place to prevent my being defrauded?

All She Wanted

And that ye will save alive my father, and my mother, and my brethren, and my sisters, and all that they have, and deliver our lives from death.
Josh. 2:13

Rahab was a hard negotiator. She went for the maximum and asked for what she really wanted. She reached out boldly and was not timid. She asked not just for her own life, but for her family, their belongings, and all that she had to be saved. Even though she was desperate and knew she was in a bad situation, she did not allow it show.

When you enter into negotiation desperate, the other party can smell blood; they know how far they can push you and they will go for it. In life, you never know what you can get until you ask. Determine what you want, and then reach for the stars. In other words, 'Go big or go home." Ask boldly, especially when you know you offer value. It is also reflected sometimes in how we plan, pray, and in our walk with God. We get so desperate that we are willing to settle for crumbs when God wants to give us a seat at the table.

God himself knows that deliverance is not complete without prosperity.

In such a situation, the sensible or 'righteous' thing for Rahab would have been to ask for just her life to be spared and be thankful. Yet Rahab had no shame about requesting for what she wanted. Being saved physically was not enough. She asked for her possessions too. She knew that when Jericho fell she was going to have to start over again, and she would need material possessions to do so. They would all need their possessions. Therefore, she asked to be saved along with everything she would need.

This same principle Moses understood in his dialogue with Pharaoh.

And Pharaoh called unto Moses, and said, Go ye, serve the LORD; only let your flocks and your herds be stayed: let your little ones also go with you. And Moses said, Thou must give us also sacrifices and burnt offerings, that we may sacrifice unto the LORD our God. Our cattle also shall go with us; there shall not an hoof be left behind...

Exo. 10:24-26

Even though the children of Israel were slaves, they would leave not just with their lives but also with all they had. God himself knows that deliverance is not complete without prosperity. And because Moses chose to demand this, God went a step further and gave them not just what was theirs but also the wealth of Egypt.

Why do Kingdom people trivialize possessions and wealth so much? Yet, this woman was basically saying, "Our lives wouldn't be worth much if we join your society as destitutes, stripped of all possessions. We need our possessions." A lot of Christians try to pretend that wealth is not useful. Settle it once and for all, money matters. While it is definitely not **everything,** even God agrees it matters. Money is a defence.

For wisdom is a defence, and money is a defence: but the excellency of knowledge is, that wisdom giveth life to them that have it.
Eccl. 7:12

Rahab followed this same principle. "If my life should be spared, I would also not go out empty."

Clear Terms of Agreement

It is amazing when I listen to people's business proposals and find out that many have not thought about when to invoice. An invoice is clear terms of the agreement between both parties before the transaction can begin. It is also documented. A lot of people do not even have a model for invoicing in their businesses.

In your restaurant, are you sure you have a diligent and solid model to ensure people pay when they are done with eating? As a caterer, do you cater for the wedding before you get paid? In building your business model, be sure to make it clear at which point people are meant to pay for your goods and services or deliver their end of the bargain. You would be surprised at how many people attempt to conduct serious business with no expectations and deliverables clearly stated from each party.

… God went a step further and gave them not just what was theirs, but also the wealth of Egypt.

Rahab asked for a detailed agreement. It was to be clear what they were to do in return for what she was to do. She knew exactly when to invoice: that was before the goods would be used and value extracted. There was a **Promisee** (the one to whom the promise is made to), a **Promisor** (the one who makes the promise or contractual agreement), and a **Consideration** (compensation given by a promisor pending when the **performance** is completed).

Rahab knew what to look for as deliverables in enforcing performance. She stated and was very clear on the terms before she made them comfortable.

A Token

Now therefore, I pray you, swear unto me by the Lord, since I have shewed you kindness, that ye will also shew kindness unto my father's house, and give me a true token.

Josh. 2:12

Creating an invoice is one thing. Having it followed is another. This is more probable when a token of goodwill is involved; call it a deposit if you will. It has to cost the buyer and be important to them.

In the case of the spies, Rahab asked for a token after agreements had been reached. By taking this step she demonstrated her understanding of the business culture. While conducting international transactions across cross-cultural lines, she asked for a surety rooted in the values and mores her business partners respected. What was important to them? Jehovah. That was **Who** they served. Rahab did not serve Jehovah even though she had heard of Him. She knew how important He was to the Israelites and how much He was feared by them. Therefore, to ensure their compliance, she made them swear not by her own belief system but by what they held sacred.

This is such an important principle. When studying drafts of contracts as an architect and an arbitrator, I know it is important to state which laws govern the transaction, and not just the contract but also any further dispute resolution that results from the contract. Language is an important tool of communication. In the marketplace, it is important to understand the language and literature of the corridors of power, the mountains you seek to take or the kingdom you seek to penetrate.

In the book of Daniel, the king instructs Asphenaz, the chief of the eunuchs, to recruit young men who could be taught the 'language and literature of the Chaldeans'.

In the marketplace, it is important to understand the language and literature of the corridors of power, the mountains you seek to take or the kingdom you seek to penetrate.

Young men in whom there was no blemish, but good-looking, gifted in all wisdom, possessing knowledge and quick to understand, who had ability to serve in the king's palace, and whom they might teach the language and literature of the Chaldeans.

Daniel 1:4

Let us pause here for a bit. The term *'language and literature'* is a weighty one. **Language** refers to a means of communication and stretches to communicating thoughts, ideas, and instructions. However, **Literature** goes deeper. It describes the culture, mores, values, and principles of a society. In dealing with cultures, as a result, you must realise that when you transgress the mores of a culture or bridge a laid-down principle or law, it is difficult to find favour in the eyes of that culture. Therefore, favour can actually be procured by understanding the environment you are dealing with, regardless of what your own native culture is.

To go far in another culture, you must understand the native culture. This the king wanted in the education of the Hebrew children. This is similar to learning Japanese to conduct business within a Japanese market. You find, when people get to Japan and have to do business with the Japanese, they bow. You can choose not to bow at the risk of losing the business, but most pragmatic people realise that it costs nothing to bow and they do so regardless of their personal belief system.

While this is important, there are things in each culture all over the world which are against the word of God and things which are innocuous. In making important decisions, we turn to the word of God always as a final arbiter.

Chapter 9

PRINCIPLE VIII
Influence

Now therefore, I pray you, swear unto me by the LORD, since I have shewed you kindness, that ye will also shew kindness unto my father's house, and give me a true token: and that ye will save alive my father, and my mother, and my brethren, and my sisters, and all that they have, and deliver our lives from death.

Josh. 2:3

Being wealthy has its value. Wealth creates limitless opportunities, some of which include options, choices, platforms, and ultimately influence. Apart from some exceptions – monks, nuns, hermits, ascetic individuals - a lot of us believe that if you are competent and excel in what you are doing, you should also be wealthy to a certain degree.

Wealth has become a determinant of success and we usually equate wealth with success and with competence. When people excel in their place of assignment and prosper we also give them the opportunity to speak into our lives. Think of the many times we invite wealthy people to speak to us.

However, with all that can be said about wealth, wealth is really currency for **Influence**. Rahab's business activities and wealth, as well as her investments in the lives of others, had without a doubt brought her into a place of influence over her family and within Jericho. Her influence was demonstrated by the fact that:

- As stated earlier, she was known by the king. This could have stemmed from the businesses she ran which might have had some top clientele and which made her also a wealthy woman.

- Her house was situated 'upon the town wall and she dwelt upon the wall'. (Josh. 2:15): This was no ordinary location. She had to be trusted to be allowed to site her house in such a sensitive place where she could create a breach in the city's defences. Only someone with great influence could be allowed in that position of trust.

- She could gather her whole household into her home. How large was her house? How could she persuade them all to come under her roof with all they had, and in such patriarchal times? And they indeed obeyed. I believe this could not have been the first time this was happening. If it was, it would have been a tough call to have them all obey. How did she gather them all under her roof without explaining why she was doing so? Bear in mind, this gathering had to be effected with discretion as she had been told not to tell anyone about the 'business.' (I actually find it instructive that both parties understood clearly that the instruction was a business and a clear transaction.)

And the men answered her, Our life for yours, if ye utter not this our business. And it shall be, when the LORD hath given us the land, that we will deal kindly and truly with thee... And if thou utter this our business, then we will be quit of thine oath which thou hast made us to swear.

Josh. 2:14, 20

You cannot wield influence where you have no investment.

Without a doubt, it certainly was not a rarity to have such assembling of the entire extended family under Rahab's roof. She was clearly a hospitable woman whose influence pervaded her household, obviously as a result of her tangible investments in their lives. She had used her opportunities and platform to benefit not just herself alone, but also the larger group. She wasn't just focused only on building or caring for herself. She did same for others.

Now therefore, I pray you, swear unto me by the LORD, since I have shewed you kindness, that ye will also shew kindness unto my father's house, and give me a true token: and that ye will save alive my father, and my mother, and my brethren, and my sisters, and all that they have, and deliver our lives from death.

Josh. 2:12-13

Her immediately negotiating with the spies for her family as well showed that this was instinctive - keeping her entire, extended family safe and cared for at all times. It was second nature to her and must have been something she had done often and often again. Obviously, she had enough space in her home to habitually accommodate them, thus allowing her play that role easily when the time came.

How many people eat at your table? How many benefit from your largesse? Have you ever sponsored a scholar that's not your own child? What have you done for those who don't seem to have the means to ever return the favour? Examine your account statement. Where is your money going? The destination of your money/investment is the target and scope of your influence. You cannot wield influence where you have no investment.

Investment precedes influence. To speak into my life you must have first invested in my life. It is very rare for people to follow those who have not invested or helped them in any way. You obey your boss not because of the 'boss' title or because you like him/her. No. You obey because he/she offers you an incentive or pays you a salary.

When you don't invest in people, you cannot influence them. When your life impacts others, you are able to tell them what to do and they will listen. Who are you influencing? Who is listening to you? In the days ahead, we must understand the role of influence in propagating the Kingdom and preserving the body of Christ.

Without a doubt, Rahab must have invested in her family. As a result, when the time came for her to obey the agreement entered into with the spies she was able to get their compliance and have them follow her without divulging the secret. It took a man of wealth and influence, Joseph of Arimathea, to obtain the body of Christ from Pontius Pilate. Prayer couldn't do it, the Apostles couldn't. Wealth and influence did.

When the even was come, there came a rich man of Arimathaea, named Joseph, who also himself was Jesus' disciple: He went to Pilate, and begged the body of Jesus. Then Pilate commanded the body to be delivered.

Matt. 27:57-59

And now when the even was come, because it was the preparation, that is, the day before the sabbath, Joseph of Arimathaea, an honourable counsellor, which also waited for the kingdom of God, came, and went in boldly unto Pilate, and craved the body of Jesus.

And Pilate marvelled if he were already dead: and calling unto him the centurion, he asked him whether he had been any while dead. And when he knew it of the centurion, he gave the body to Joseph. And he bought fine linen, and took him down, and wrapped him in the linen, and laid him in a sepulchre which was hewn out of a rock, and rolled a stone unto the door of the sepulchre.

Mk. 15:42-46

In the days ahead we must understand the role of influence in propagating the Kingdom and preserving the body of Christ.

And, behold, there was a man named Joseph, a counsellor; and he was a good man, and a just: (The same had not consented to the counsel and deed of them;) he was of Arimathaea, a city of the Jews: who also himself waited for the kingdom of God.

This man went unto Pilate, and begged the body of Jesus. And he took it down, and wrapped it in linen, and laid it in a sepulchre that was hewn in stone, wherein never man before was laid.
Luk. 23:50-53

The order in which the Bible states facts is deliberate. Joseph is described as a rich man first before his name is even mentioned. He could access the Roman Governor who ultimately listened to and heeded him. This was not just because he was rich but because he served and led in the community as a counsellor, a member of the Sanhedrin most likely. It is not enough to be rich. To have influence, you must lead and serve.

In the excerpt from the book of Luke we see that Joseph placed the body of Jesus in a tomb where no one had ever been laid. Only the rich could afford rock-hewn tombs. It had been prophesied that Jesus would be laid in a rich man's tomb.

And he made his grave with the wicked, and with the rich in his death; because he had done no violence, neither was any deceit in his mouth.
Is. 53:9

The role Joseph of Arimathea, the rich counsellor and disciple who looked for the Kingdom, played in God's agenda is dumbfounding. No matter how the poor loved Jesus, only a rich man could have fulfilled this prophecy. Only a rich and influential man could have accessed Pilate to request for the body. Without the body being preserved for Jesus' spirit to return into after three days in hell, the work of redemption would never have been completed.

And in these last days, influence and wealth will also preserve the body of Christ.

What if the body had been thrown in some dump or pit and the dogs had gotten to it? What if it had been cremated for sanitation's sake? Where would the women have gone on resurrection morning? Where would the angel who rolled the stone away have sat? On the trash heap? I have been blessed to visit the conventionally accepted site of Jesus' tomb several times from my youth and it is situated in what was proven archeologically to be a rich man's garden. The tomb is befitting and provides even in its emptiness the evidence we need of Christ's resurrection. And in these last days, influence and wealth will also preserve the body of Christ (the Church).

Chapter 10

PRINCIPLE IX
Perseverance

Behold, when we come into the land, thou shalt bind this line of scarlet thread in the window which thou didst let us down by: and thou shalt bring thy father, and thy mother, and thy brethren, and all thy father's household, home unto thee. And she said, According unto your words, so be it. And she sent them away, and they departed: and she bound the scarlet line in the window.

Josh. 2:18, 21

The instructions were simple. The most important being that as soon as she heard the Israelites advance towards Jericho Rahab would tie a scarlet thread on her window which could be easily seen by them. She was given no timeline or deadline for when the spies would reappear. Yet, she was 'extra' since she didn't know when the spies would return or if she would get the news of their return in a timely manner. As soon as the spies departed she immediately put up the scarlet thread.

I am sure when she tied the scarlet thread to her window a storm might have come to tear it away, or someone who did not know the reason for it may have reached out through their windows to pull it down. A lot of things might have happened to the original scarlet thread. But Rahab maintained that scarlet thread in her window, watching and persevering daily with consistency to ensure that the status of the thread was not threatened.

Are you persevering in the things you have been born to do, or you do it halfway because of some criticism or squabble between you and your business partner? Have you let go of your work ethic? Millions of reasons would always come along to adjust the playing field. Yet, like Rahab, you have to maintain consistency in the absence of no motivation.

You have to learn to be self-motivated, focused on the end in mind, regardless of how you feel or changing situations.

Some people do well when they are being motivated 24 hours, 7 days a week. When they do not get the motivation they seek they cannot keep up the tempo. We have to learn to be focused on the end goal and self-motivated, regardless of how we feel or changing situations.

And David was greatly distressed; for the people spake of stoning him, because the soul of all the people was grieved, every man for his sons and for his daughters: but David encouraged himself in the Lord his God.

1 Samuel 30:6

As depicted in the verse above by David, real leaders know how to motivate themselves. Beyond building the skill needed to build your business, learn to build yourself up. Learn to function without external validation and be motivated by your purpose. Understand that your job is not just a job but an assignment. Understand that your business is more than a profit-making venture. It is an assignment. So, when the market does not encourage you, when people do not encourage you, when clients do not encourage you, you must be encouraged by the vision that you saw from the beginning.

This is why it is important that we have a vision when we go into business, when we take up a job, or when we take up an assignment. We must know why we are here. We do not take up a job just because of a salary. In the same vein, we do not start a business because it looks profitable. Everything we do must be by revelation. We need to be consistent in the absence of external spurs, external motivation, external provocation. Can you keep at an assignment when you don't know how long it will take? Can you continue to work on the assignments you have been given?

Rahab stayed where she was told to and obeyed each instruction. But how was she able to? She learnt to stay hopeful and remain trusting. She could have doubted they would honour their agreement with her or even return. It wouldn't be anything new. After all, in her line of work she was used to many disappointments. We know prostitutes are exposed to many dangers. From perverts to traffickers, procurers, and various hazards. Yet, despite her history, she remained open, not cynical, and was willing to trust again.

I am blessed to be a Nigerian. We are a country of over 190 million mostly hospitable, kind, intelligent, well-read, and extremely-resourceful people. In the city of Lagos, which is our commercial hub, we have more Harvard PhD holders than in any other city in the world. However, the press about the country outside Nigeria is about how we are scammers, advanced fee fraudsters, and other awful things. These persons represent a tiny fraction of Nigerians.

I recall a time a country was having a 'Nigerian problem.' Their prisons were full of Nigerians and they had to come to Nigeria to study what was going on. They were able to trace these problems to just one ethnic group. As a result, they had to study the culture and thinking of that ethnic community. This country was interested enough to tell the difference between Nigerians.

Avoid being drawn into generalizations. All people are not the same. The fact that someone from a particular group, ethnicity, or tribe hurt you does not mean another from the same ethnic group won't become your friend and your greatest source of joy. Some have been hurt and closed themselves to new beginnings. Some have written off the entire male gender. Perhaps it's the pain of a broken relationship, perhaps it's the pain of a divorce, perhaps it's the pain of being scammed in business. The Yorubas have a saying, "If you close your eyes because you do not want to see evil people, when good people pass by you also will not see them." If you close your heart because of someone who hurt you, you also close your heart to joy.

Remain open. Learn from the encounters you have, but remain open. Regardless of how much you have been hurt, you must learn from the hurts and must try again. Over and over, learn to rise up and try again. Every day is a new beginning, and God's mercies and blessings are new every morning.

In the same vein, we cannot start a business because it looks profitable. Everything we do must be by revelation.

It is of the LORD'S mercies that we are not consumed, because his compassions fail not. They are new every morning: great is thy faithfulness.

Lam 3:22-23

CONCLUSION

There Is A Reward

When Rahab embarked on this journey, her goal was to save herself and her extended family (which comprised of many others). But in her quest to do this, she ended up aligning herself with God's purposes.

Many are the plans in a man's heart but the counsel of the Lord that shall stand.
Prov. 19:21

To be quite honest, many of us do not know God is not interested in our agenda. He is interested in His. Hannah, who was going to come afterwards, aligned herself with God's purpose by saying, "God, you need a priest, I need a son. Give me a son and he can be your priest."

Rahab never knew that in conforming to God's plan and purposes, she was going to reap many incredible blessings.

First: She was saved along with her family.

And Joshua saved Rahab the harlot alive, and her father's household…
Josh. 6:25

Second: She experienced no loss. Everything she had was preserved.

And Joshua saved Rahab the harlot alive, and her father's household, and ***all that she had...***
Josh. 6:25

To be quite honest many of us do not know that God is not interested in our agenda – He is interested in His.

Third: She was adopted immediately into the chosen family of God. She could have been sent to a different city like Lot was when Sodom and Gomorrah were being destroyed. Isn't it unusual that Lot wasn't told to return to Abraham with whom God had made a covenant to build a people? Maybe he would have been a distraction to Abraham and derailed the promise. Yet Rahab had a greater privilege: room was made for her and her family, and she was automatically welcomed and grafted into the family of God.

...and she dwelleth in Israel even unto this day; because she hid the messengers, which Joshua sent to spy out Jericho.
Josh. 6:25

Fourth: She became a wife and mother. After beginning life anew among God's people, Rahab also became married and bore Boaz. He would become the great-grandfather of David the king.

And Salmon begat Booz of Rachab; and Booz begat Obed of Ruth; and Obed begat Jesse; And Jesse begat David the king.
Matt. 1:5-6

Fifth: She was listed in Hebrews among the heroes of faith.

By faith the harlot Rahab perished not with them that believed not, when she had received the spies with peace.
Heb. 11:31

Here, we see a great ending to this story and may not know what qualities Rahab possessed that took her this far. Do not be deceived. For every lifting and promotion there are two parts – God's part and our part. We only have control over our part of the miracle. But when we fulfil our own part, God moves sovereignly and fulfils His.

In regards to the part we have the ability to affect, man's part, we see how important Rahab's business acumen was, how momentous her generosity, her influence, and the knowledge of her business partners were. We have seen how important her negotiating skills, discretion, diligence, and her ability to read trends and forecasts were.

We have also studied how significant her knowledge of history was, how essential it was that she could apply wisdom to her knowledge, the significance of her switching allegiance, her discernment, her ability to remain open, her prompt actions, and her perseverance. All these traits played huge parts until the very end.

Like Rahab, who translated from being a mere woman to an institution we read about in history books today, our little contributions to society and to the marketplace have the potential to be appreciated through the ages and aeons to come.

However, if we start with that in mind, we may not achieve much.

Do not be deceived; in every miracle there are two parts – God's part and man's part.

But seek ye first the kingdom of God, and his righteousness; and all these things shall be added unto you.
Matt. 6:33

If we start with God in mind, the future is guaranteed. Our lives will leave an impact on many, and we will become role models for future generations to come. When Steve Jobs designed his first computer little did he know that this book would be typed on a Mac book today.

Where are you today? Where you will be in the next 10-20 years is going to be a result of the decisions you take today. We make decisions, and these decisions turn around and then make us. Starting from this hour, the decision to read this book, the decision to repent from every form of prostitution as Rahab invariably did in taking the decision to leave Jericho and consequently her way of life in Jericho, the decision to upgrade, to up-skill, the decision to take that first step in your career or business might be the first drop in the ocean that will reverberate and touch many generations.

There is a reward. We are called to the marketplace to affect the world for God and called to possess and transform our particular pillars – Government, Media, Business, Education, Arts and Entertainment, Family, Science - for the kingdom of God.

Which is your pillar or platform of influence?

About the Author

Olajumoke Adenowo (Arc) is a multiple award-winning architect with over three decades of industry experience. Described as Africa's 'Starchitect' and trailblazer when profiled by CNN and BBC, she is one of Africa's most outstanding architects and the only female in this elite category. Christened the **Face of Architecture in Nigeria** by the Guardian, she has been featured in the world's foremost architectural journal Architectural Record and in Forbes Women and Fortune magazine.

In 2013, she was instituted into the Hall of Fame of **Personalities of Black Ancestry** by the University of West England, Bristol, among other global personalities of black heritage.

Olajumoke gained admission into Obafemi Awolowo University, Ile-Ife, at the age of fourteen, and she acquired the first distinction in Masters of Science in Architecture in the University's history. She is also an alumnus of a number of prestigious institutions including the Harvard Kennedy School of Government, the Yale School of Management, the IESE Business School amongst others. She is a member of the

Institute of Chartered Arbitrators (UK) and a Fellow of the Nigerian Institute of Architects.

Olajumoke started her career at Femi Majekodunmi Associates, where she had the privilege of designing the Federal Ministry of Finance Headquarters in Abuja. In 1994, she founded her own multi-award-winning architecture firm, AD Consulting, which specialises also in the master planning of eco-sensitive developments. AD Consulting is Nigeria's most internationally awarded firm. She has been the principal partner from inception to date.

In 1999, Olajumoke's passion for raising transformational leaders led her to establish the faith-based philanthropy, Awesome Treasures Foundation. It is recognized by the United Nations and affiliated to the Edmond De Rothschild Foundation Family Philanthropy Platform. Awesome Treasures Foundation is established on three continents with initiatives impacting millions.

She is the pioneer recipient of the **New African Women in Business Award**, has been recognised as one of Africa's **'Top Ten Most Powerful Women in Business'**, one of **Nigeria's Most Inspiring Women**, one of Nigeria's **100 most Influential Nigerians**, the International Alliance for Women **World of Difference 100 Award**, as well as one of the **Most Inspiring Women in Nigeria** amongst other honours.

Olajumoke Adenowo was the recipient of the **2019 Leadership Award** by the Constituency For Africa (Washington, DC). In 2019 she was appointed a visiting professor at Germany's Leading Architecture program, Technische Universitat Munchen (TUM) in Germany. She was honoured as a Laureate and Guest Scientist at the Chair of Theory, History of Architecture and Art & Design.

Adenowo is a speaker of note at summits and conferences, and has spoken at several global platforms, including the Global Women's Forum, Harvard Business School's Africa Business Club, Cambridge University's African Society, and SOLVE MIT's flagship conference for global thought leaders and innovators. She is a minister of the gospel, and member of The International Coalition of Apostolic Leaders. She hosts her own syndicated radio program, Voice of Change on Leadership.

Olajumoke has served on juries and panels of global initiatives such as The Cartier Initiative for Women Awards. She has authored several books, including *Life Spring, Mysterious Seed*, *Appointment With Destiny,* and *Beyond My Dreams*.

She is married to Olukorede and they are blessed with two men.

Printed in Great Britain
by Amazon

41754678R00061